FUN
Sports
FOR FITNESS

HUNTING

Written by

Julie K. Lundgren

Educational Media

rourkeeducationalmedia.com

*Scan for Related Titles
and Teacher Resources*

www.rourkeeducationalmedia.com

PHOTO CREDITS: Cover © Susie Prentice; Title Page © Indigo Fish; Page 4 © Ihoop; Page 5 © DIGIcal; Page 6 © Ivan Montero Martinez; Page 7 © GTibbetts, Vadim Kozlovsky; Page 8 © Koerpers; Page 9 © Bodil1955; Page 10 © Vladi; Page 11 © Mike Cherim; Page 12 © Nate Allred; Page 13 © Troy Kellogg; Page 14 © Steve Oehlesnschlager; Page 15 © faslooff; Page 16 © Blue Door Publishing; Page 17 © Tony Campbell; Page 18 © MidwestWilderness; Page 19 © beachnet; Page 20 © eurobanks; Page 21 © Jeff Banke; Page 22 © Pedro Jorge Henriques Monteiro

Editor: Jill Sherman

Cover Designer: Tara Raymo

Interior Designer:Jen Thomas

Library of Congress PCN Data

Hunting / Julie K.Lundgren
Fun Sports for Fitness
  ISBN 978-1-62169-861-6 (hardcover)
  ISBN 978-1-62169-756-5 (softcover)
  ISBN 978-1-62169-963-7 (e-Book)
Library of Congress Control Number: 2013936466

Also Available as:
ROURKE'S
e-Books

Rourke Educational Media
Printed in the United States of America,
North Mankato, Minnesota

Rourke
Educational Media

rourkeeducationalmedia.com

customerservice@rourkeeducationalmedia.com • PO Box 643328 Vero Beach, Florida 32964

TABLE OF CONTENTS

THE TRADITION OF HUNTING

People have hunted animals throughout human history. People today hunt for many reasons. The satisfaction of providing food for the table, the challenge and excitement of the chase, and family tradition bring new hunters to the sport every year.

Landowners who like to hunt often try to improve the **habitat** on their land so more or larger animals can live there successfully.

TOP TIP

Gun use in hunting is typically regulated by the game category, area within the state, and time period.

WEAPONRY

Hunters match the weapon to the animal they are hunting and the hunting **season**. Rifles, each made for a specific size of **ammunition**, are commonly used for hunting. Hunters use larger ammunition for deer, bear, elk, and other large animals. They use smaller ammunition for small **game** like rabbits and squirrels. Bird hunters favor shotguns, which allow them to hit small, speedy targets.

Rifles fire with great accuracy over a long distance. Shotguns fire a shell filled with small metal pellets, called shot, over short distances. Hunters also use **slugs** in shotguns. Slugs make the shotgun perform more like a rifle and can be used on large game.

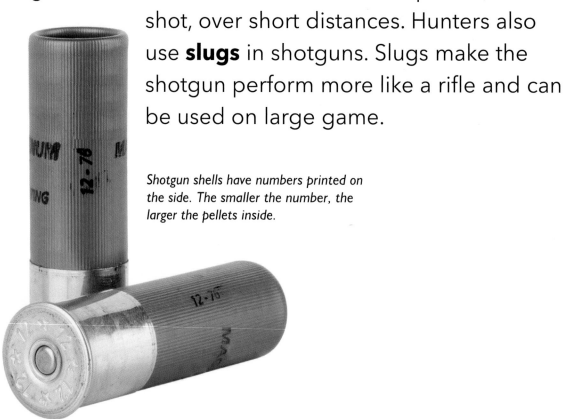

Shotgun shells have numbers printed on the side. The smaller the number, the larger the pellets inside.

Shotgun

sight

barrel

chamber

muzzle

action

guard

trigger

stock

Using a bow and arrow offers the hunter a special challenge. Because bows shoot shorter distances than guns, bowhunters must be much closer to their target animal. Wild animals frighten easily. Bowhunters need to use all their patience and skills to remain quiet, unseen, steady, and focused on the shot.

Bows come in different styles and sizes. Traditional **archers** may use longbows, recurve bows, or other styles. Other hunters prefer compound bows, which allow the user to fire arrows greater distances with more power. Compound bows, because they have many moving parts, can fail more often than simpler traditional bows.

Most bowhunters hunt for whitetail deer while some hunt for caribou, elk, and bear.

TOP TIP

Guns use gunpowder for power. Bowhunters provide power for shooting arrows by bending the arms, or limbs, of the bow.

HOMEWORK FOR HUNTING

Successful hunters learn as much as they can about their **quarry**. They study the kind of habitat it prefers and how the animal meets its needs for daily living. They look for animal **signs**, such as tracks, trails, or other evidence that show the animal lives there. Knowing the animal helps hunters locate it in the field.

Know the laws that apply to the **harvest** of the target animal. Rule books will tell you how many animals may be taken, the time of year they may be hunted, and what kind of animals are legal to be hunted. The laws about **licenses** and youth hunting differ from state to state. Check with your state's fish and wildlife department to learn more.

Fresh snow offers a lot of advantages to hunters. Deer can be tracked in fresh snow by anyone regardless of experience.

TOP TIP

Tracking in hunting is the science and art of being able to recognize and follow animals through their tracks, signs, and trails.

TOP TIP

Scouting an area is an
important part of hunting. It
gives the hunter an advantage
over their game by knowing
where and when to enter.

Well before the season starts, many hunters scout the land. They search for animal watering and feeding areas, animal tracks and trails, and resting places. They also look for the sneakiest places to enter the hunting area. Hunted animals learn where to expect trouble and stay away from those places.

Not everyone owns good hunting land. **Public land** offers opportunities for everyone. Public land managers can provide maps and share advice with hunters on the rules, regulations, and best places to find game in the area.

Hunters wishing to hunt on private land should get permission from the landowner.

RESPONSIBILITY AND SAFETY

Hunters must hunt safely and responsibly. Many states offer firearm and bowhunting safety training. They teach everything from hunting and shooting skills to hunting laws and survival skills.

The top safety rules for guns include the following:

- Always treat a gun as if it is loaded with ammunition and could fire at any time.

- Keep the **safety** on and your finger off the trigger until just before shooting.

- Never point a weapon at anything you do not want to shoot.

- Be sure of your target and the location of your hunting partners.

- Unload the gun before climbing a tree or crossing a fence or stream.

- Unload the gun before placing it in a vehicle.

The top safety rules for bowhunters include the following:

- Use caution when handling and carrying arrows.

- Never shoot an arrow straight up into the air.

- Never climb while carrying your weapon.

Hunters have a responsibility to respect others and nature. The best hunters honor game animals and the sport by not littering, taking only the animals they will eat or use, and avoiding practices that do not allow animals a fair chance.

Since an arrow will not fly as far as a bullet, bowhunters often have an easier time getting permission from landowners to hunt on their land.

TOP TIP

Hunting for trophy animals requires extra preparation. Trophies tend to be older, smarter animals with lots of experience avoiding hunters.

THE THRILL OF THE HUNT

Hunters dress carefully for the weather and the type of hunt. Bowhunters and duck hunters often dress in **camouflage** clothing, while others rely on the safety of blaze orange, an extremely bright color that allows them to be seen easily by other hunters.

TOP TIP

Fluorescent orange clothing has become standard equipment for hunters. It prevents other hunters from mistaking a person for an animal, or shooting in your direction.

The large, open lands of the western United States make it difficult for hunters to sit and wait for large game like mule deer. Hunters there prefer to spot animals from great distances using tree stands and binoculars, and then move in just close enough to shoot.

Duck, turkey, and deer hunters sometimes use **calls** to locate a target animal or bring it closer. Once an animal moves into shooting distance, the hunter may shoot. To avoid animal suffering, hunters only take shots they think they can make. If they wound an animal, they take responsibility for finishing the kill. Immediately after the kill, hunters often remove the animal's guts to allow the body to cool more quickly and avoid spoiled meat. It also makes the animal lighter to carry.

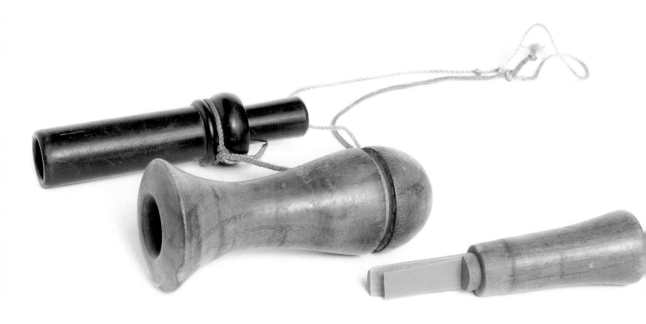

In old times, a duck call was a very simple woodwind instrument. From 1900-1910 many modifications were made to duck calls such as using materials other than wood, like rubber and acrylic.

TOP TIP

Laws sometimes allow the use of animal models, called decoys, to bring game within shooting distance.

Hunters love their sport and want to help take care of the land and its animals. Hunting clubs and organizations teach others about hunting and creating good animal habitats. Many hunters support conservation efforts to protect animal species for future generations. Hunters and other nature lovers can then enjoy wildlife and continue the hunting tradition for many years to come.

GLOSSARY

ammunition (am-yu-NIH-shun): bullets or shot loaded into a weapon

archers (AR-cherz): people who use bows and arrows, for either hunting or target competition

calls (KAHLZ): tools that hunters use to sound like the kind of animal being hunted

camouflage (KAM-uh-flahzh): coloring or shape that allows someone or something to blend in with its surroundings

game (GAYM): animals hunted for sport or food

habitat (HAB-uh-tat): an animal's natural home, which provides for all its needs

harvest (HAR-vehst): the killing of animals for human use

licenses (LYE-sehn-sehz): permits sold to someone so they can do an activity, like hunting and fishing

public land (PUHB-lick LAND): land open for use by all the people of an area, often managed by a government agency

quarry (KWOR-ee): the animal or prey that a hunter seeks

safety (SAYF-tee): a device on a firearm that locks the trigger so the gun cannot fire

season (SEE-zuhn): a period of time when hunting certain animals with certain weapons is allowed by law

signs (SINEZ): evidence an animal has left behind, such as tracks, waste, scratches on the ground or on trees, and nibbled plants

slugs (SLUHGZ): single lumps of metal that act as bullets for shotguns

INDEX

WEBSITES TO VISIT

www.youthoutdoorsusa.com/kids_hunting_websites.htm

kidsgonehunting.com

www.ducks.org

SHOW WHAT YOU KNOW

1. What is the purpose of wearing orange vests while hunting?

2. How do decoys help when hunting?

3. Can you hunt on private land without getting permission first?

4. What do hunters need to consider when selecting their weapon?

5. What makes hunting with a bow and arrow different than using a gun?